Jonah

A THREE-WEEK STUDY

goodmorninggirls.org

Jonah

© 2025 Women Living Well Ministries, LLC

More Bible Studies

from Courtney & WomenLivingWell.org

Ecclesiastes: Wisdom for Living Well
6 Week In-Depth Study

Ruth: God's Amazing Love for You
5 Week In-Depth Study

Life Rhythms That Bring Rest
A 4-Week Guide to Making Your Home a Haven

Making Your Home a Haven
4-Week Bible Study

Rest and Release
4-Week Bible Study

Slowing Down for Spiritual Growth
4-Week Bible Study

Delight in the Lord
4-Week Bible Study

Don't Let Go! Holding Onto God When You Feel Like *Giving Up, 31-Day Prayer Journal*

Resting in His Presence
4-Week Bible Study on the Names of Jesus

Peace, Be Still
31-Day Christmas Prayer Journal

Hosanna in the Highest
A 4-Week Journey to the Cross & the Risen King

Summer in the Psalms
Bible Word Searches: Volume 1, 2 & 3

Books of the Bible

Study Journals

Numbers	1 Kings	Job	Mark	Galatians
Deuteronomy	2 Kings	Psalms	Luke	Ephesians
Joshua	1 Chronicles	Proverbs	John	Philippians
Judges	2 Chronicles	Ecclesiastes	Acts	Colossians
Ruth	Ezra	Isaiah	Romans	James
1 Samuel	Nehemiah	Jeremiah	1 Corinthians	
2 Samuel		Hosea	2 Corinthians	

and more to come...

Join the GMG Community

Use hashtag **#WomenLivingWell**
& share your daily SOAK on...

f Facebook.com/**GoodMorningGirlsWLW**

⃝ Instagram.com/**WomenLivingWell**

Welcome to Good Morning Girls! We are so glad you are joining us.

God created us to walk with Him, to know Him, and to be loved by Him. He is our living well, and when we drink from the water He continually provides, His living water will change the entire course of our lives.

Jesus said: "Whoever drinks of the water that I will give him will never be thirsty again. The water that I will give him will become in him a spring of water welling up to eternal life." ~ Johns 4:14 (ESV)

So let's begin! The method we use here at GMG is called the SOAK method.

S Scripture
Read the chapter for the day. Then choose 1-2 verses and write them out word for word. (There is no right or wrong choice — just let the Holy Spirit guide you.)

O Observation
Look at the verse or verses you wrote out. Write 1 or 2 observations. What stands out to you? What do you learn about the character of God from these verses? Is there a promise, command or teaching?

A Application
Personalize the verses. What is God saying to you? How can you apply them to your life? Are there any changes you need to make or an action to take?

K Kneeling in Prayer
Pause, kneel and pray. Confess any sin God has revealed to you today. Praise God for His word. Pray the passage over your own life or someone you love. Ask God to help you live out your applications.

SOAK God's word into your heart and squeeze every bit of nourishment you can out of each day's scripture reading. Soon you will find your life transformed by the renewing of your mind! Walk with the King!

Courtney

WomenLivingWell.org | GoodMorningGirls.org

GMG Bible Coloring Chart

COLORS	KEY WORDS
PURPLE	God, Jesus, Holy Spirit, Saviour, Messiah
PINK	women of the Bible, family, marriage, parenting, friendship, relationships
RED	love, kindness, mercy, compassion, peace, grace
GREEN	faith, obedience, growth, fruit, salvation, fellowship, repentance
YELLOW	worship, prayer, praise, doctrine, angels, miracles, power of God, blessings
BLUE	wisdom, teaching, instruction, commands
ORANGE	prophecy, history, times, places, kings, genealogies, people, numbers, covenants, vows, visions, oaths, future
GRAY	Satan, sin, death, hell, evil, idols, false teachers, hypocrisy, temptation

INTRODUCTION TO THE
Book of Jonah

I The book of Jonah is considered one of the twelve books of the Minor Prophets and yet it is unlike any of the other prophetic books. Rather than a series of messages from God, the book of Jonah is a short story of Jonah's attempt to run from God. This book teaches us important lessons of grace, mercy, second chances, and listening to God's call.

God called Jonah to take his message of judgment to Nineveh and he refused. This resulted in him being swallowed by a great fish! After three days, the fish spit Jonah out onto dry land and only then did Jonah obey the Lord and deliver God's message to the Ninevites.

What is interesting to note is that the chief god that the Ninevites worshipped was Dagon. The idol Dagon was depicted as half man and half fish, making the fact that Jonah survived three days in the belly of a fish truly remarkable and likely very significant to the Ninevite people. Also noteworthy is the fact that Jonah is the only prophetic book in which a prophet was sent to a gentile nation.

THE PURPOSE The book of Jonah not only illustrates Jonah's disobedience and repentance but contrasts the immediate repentance of the Ninevite people to the stubborn rebellion of Israel and Judah. While Jonah was carrying God's message to Nineveh, prophets were also sent to Israel and Judah calling them to repentance. The Ninevites immediately repented in sackcloth and ashes, calling for a 3-day fast of all men and animals, while God's people stubbornly turned a deaf ear to God's warning. God's response to both Jonah's and Nineveh's repentance is love, mercy, and grace.

THE AUTHOR Jonah

TIME PERIOD Between 793-758 B.C.

KEY VERSE **Jonah 1:17—**"And the Lord appointed a great fish to swallow up Jonah. And Jonah was in the belly of the fish three days and three nights."

THE OUTLINE

1. **Jonah Flees from God (1)**
   A great fish swallows Jonah (1:17)
2. **Jonah in the Belly of the Fish (2)**
   Jonah Prays to God and Repents (2:2-9)
   The Fish Spits Jonah Out onto Land (2:10)
3. **Jonah Delivers God's Word (3)**
   The Ninevites Repent (3:5-9)
   God Relents and Spares Nineveh (3:10)
4. **Jonah is Angry (4)**

The book of Jonah tells the story of Jonah's futile attempt to run and hide from God, but it also carries an important lesson for us today. We may try to run from God, but we cannot hide from him. No matter where we go, God sees us, and he will not stop reaching out to us with his love, mercy and grace as long as we live.

Because of this grace we have received, God wants all of us to be messengers to those around us so that they, too, can have a second chance. His will is that no one would perish but that all would reach repentance. (2 Peter 3:9)

So, let's get started studying His word. Be sure to set aside at least 15 minutes a day for your reading. I can't wait to see how God reveals himself personally to each of us, as we read the book of Jonah together.

Keep walking with the King,

Courtney

Reading Plan

WEEK ONE

- ☐ **DAY ONE**   Jonah 1:1-3
- ☐ **DAY TWO**   Jonah 1: 4-6
- ☐ **DAY THREE**   Jonah 1:7-10
- ☐ **DAY FOUR**   Jonah 1:11-16
- ☐ **DAY FIVE**   Jonah 1:17

WEEK TWO

- ☐ **DAY ONE**   Jonah 2:1-3
- ☐ **DAY TWO**   Jonah 2:4-6
- ☐ **DAY THREE**   Jonah 2:7-9
- ☐ **DAY FOUR**   Jonah 2:10
- ☐ **DAY FIVE**   Jonah 3:1-3

WEEK THREE

- ☐ **DAY ONE**   Jonah 3:4-5
- ☐ **DAY TWO**   Jonah 3:6-10
- ☐ **DAY THREE**   Jonah 4:1-4
- ☐ **DAY FOUR**   Jonah 4:5-9
- ☐ **DAY FIVE**   Jonah 4:10-11

Week One

But Jonah rose to flee from the presence of the Lord.

JONAH 1:3

Jonah is the only Old Testament prophet called to a pagan, Gentile nation. At the time of Jonah, Nineveh was the capitol city of the Assyrian empire and the largest city in the world. The Assyrians were seeking world domination and were cruel to the cities they conquered. The wickedness of this nation was so great that God called Jonah to go to Nineveh and call them to repentance.

Jonah deeply disliked them. They had attacked Israel numerous times and were one of his most dreaded enemies. Because Jonah was a prophet of God, he knew that if they repented, God would show them mercy and not judge them for their wickedness. He did not want to risk this happening, so instead...he chose to run.

Jonah tried to run from the presence of God but that is not possible! In Psalm 139:7-8, King David says, "*Where shall I go from your Spirit? Or where shall I flee from your presence? If I ascend to heaven, you are there! If I make my bed in Sheol, you are there!*"

Have you ever tried to run from God? Perhaps like Jonah, you did not want to do what God was asking or maybe you did not feel capable of obeying. Jonah's story reminds us that though we might try to run from God, he will always find us.

Is there something you know God is calling you to, but you have been reluctant to obey? Write about it below. How does remembering that God enables those he calls encourage you today?

JONAH 1:1-3

Scripture _____

_____

_____

_____

_____

_____

Observation _____

_____

_____

_____

_____

_____

Application _____

_____

_____

_____

_____

_____

Kneeling in Prayer _____

_____

_____

_____

_____

_____

"Arise,
call out to your god!"

JONAH 1:6

This must have been a storm of supernatural proportions, because the mariners on the ship were experienced seamen. They had likely been through many storms and were not easily frightened by waves and wind. Yet, this storm made them so afraid that each man cried out to his god and even began throwing cargo overboard – the cargo that was to be for their income.

Yet in all of this, where do we find Jonah? He is asleep at the bottom of the ship. It is surprising to see how Jonah, a prophet of God, could be so unaware of the consequences of his own sin. He is sleeping peacefully and so soundly, not wakened by the horrific storm, that the captain had to wake him up and tell him to pray that God would save them.

Though not every storm in life is the result of disobedience, this is what often happens when we fail to follow through with what God has told us to do. The enemy puts blinders on our eyes so that we are unaware of the true consequences of our sin. We may personally experience those consequences, but we can't identify them for what they are. This is why disobedience to God is so serious, it opens the door for the enemy's deception in our lives.

Is there an area in your life right now where you are not fully obeying God? Why is this happening? Take a moment and surrender that area to him.

Day Two

JONAH 1:4-6

Scripture _____

_____

_____

_____

_____

Observation _____

_____

_____

_____

_____

Application _____

_____

_____

_____

_____

Kneeling in Prayer _____

_____

_____

_____

_____

"I fear the Lord, the God of heaven, who made the sea and the dry land."

JONAH 1:9

God chose to reveal Jonah's hidden sin when the seamen cast lots to determine who had caused the trouble. We see many places in the Bible where casting lots is used to determine a matter. This happened mostly in the Old Testament, and we don't see this practice used after the Day of Pentecost when the disciples were filled with the Holy Spirit.

When the lot fell on Jonah, the men asked him a series of questions to which he replied that he feared the Lord. What a contradiction to his actions! He said he feared the Lord, but he was running from the Lord.

The men called him out when they cried out in great fear, "*What is this that you have done!*" It would almost seem that they had a greater fear of God in that moment than Jonah.

When we believe we can get away with disobedience to the voice of the Lord, we fail to recognize our own hypocrisy. With our mouth we declare the greatness of God, but our actions say something else.

God's desire is that we live lives of integrity, where our actions declare to the world that we truly fear the Lord, the God of heaven, who made the sea and the dry land. Pause and consider, is there an area in your life where your actions don't show that you fear the Lord?

Day Three

JONAH 1:7–10

Scripture _____

_____

_____

_____

_____

_____

Observation _____

_____

_____

_____

_____

_____

Application _____

_____

_____

_____

_____

_____

Kneeling in Prayer _____

_____

_____

_____

_____

_____

Then the men feared the Lord exceedingly.

JONAH 1:16

As if the storm was not bad enough, it continued to grow more intense, and the mariners asked Jonah what they could do to make the sea calm again. They did not want to throw Jonah overboard. They tried to sail against the storm to dry land, but God would not allow it. The harder they sailed, the greater the storm grew in intensity until their only option was to throw Jonah into the sea.

Fearing what might happen to him, and that the Lord might judge them for their actions, they prayed that God would not judge them and then threw Jonah overboard. Miraculously, the sea calmed; and when the men saw the hand of God, they feared him.

It could not have been easy for Jonah to agree to be thrown into the sea. Surely, he thought it would be his death sentence to be thrown overboard during a storm of this magnitude. His disobedience had placed his own life, and the lives of every person on that ship, in mortal danger and the only thing left to do was to sacrifice his life to save theirs. And yet, God would be glorified, even in this. Through the storm these men's eyes were opened to see the greatness of God.

God used Jonah's brokenness to open the eyes of the sailors to see the greatness of God. He wants to use your brokenness to show His glory to a lost and dying world, too.

Is there anything in your life that causes you to struggle to see how God can use you? How does remembering that God wants to use even the hard parts of our story for his glory encourage you?

_____

_____

_____

_____

_____

_____

_____

_____

_____

Day Four

JONAH 1:11–16

Scripture _____

_____

_____

_____

_____

_____

Observation _____

_____

_____

_____

_____

_____

Application _____

_____

_____

_____

_____

_____

Kneeling in Prayer _____

_____

_____

_____

_____

_____

And the Lord appointed a great fish to swallow up Jonah. And Jonah was in the belly of the fish three days and three nights.

JONAH 1:17

While many depictions of the story of Jonah, including children's Sunday school stories, depict this fish as a whale, the Bible doesn't tell us what kind of fish swallowed Jonah. All we know is that Jonah survived being in the belly of this fish for 72 hours. This verse tells us that God prepared a fish for the very purpose to swallow Jonah, so perhaps this was a fish that God created just for this event.

In Matthew 12 and Luke 11, Jesus compares his death, burial, and resurrection to Jonah when he declared that no sign would be given to that generation except the sign of Jonah. He was referring to how he would be in the grave three days and rise again, just as Jonah was in the belly of the great fish and came out alive and well. Then Jesus said this, *"Something greater than Jonah is here"*.

Sadly, we will see a great difference in the response of the Ninevites compared to the Jews who lived and walked with the Son of God. Many people today look for signs that God is real and still active. Even Christians eagerly search for signs that God is still working.

True faith does not demand a sign. His works are all around us and his word tells us of the great works that he has done. The greatest work of all is that he sent his only son to die for our sins. Unlike Jonah, he really did die but he rose again on the third day, defeating death, hell, and the grave so we can live eternally with him! What more of a sign do we need?

If you have never received Christ as your savior, you can do that right now. Acknowledge your sin to him and your need for salvation and then purpose to live for him alone from this day forward. He loves you and he's ready and waiting to accept you into his family! For those who are saved, how has your life been transformed by God's great power?

_____

_____

_____

_____

_____

_____

Day Five

JONAH 1:17

Scripture _____

_____

_____

_____

_____

_____

Observation _____

_____

_____

_____

_____

_____

Application _____

_____

_____

_____

_____

_____

Kneeling in Prayer _____

_____

_____

_____

_____

_____

Week Two

I called out to the Lord, out of my distress, and he answered me.

JONAH 2:2

Jonah 1:17 says that Jonah was in the belly of the fish three days and three nights, and then Jonah 2:1 begins, "**Then** Jonah prayed to the Lord his God from the fish's belly." The Bible doesn't tell us what Jonah was doing during those three days and nights, but it appears that his prayer didn't begin until after three days and nights had passed!

Jonah clearly had many of the Psalms memorized, because much of his prayer is quoted from the Psalms. In today's reading, we see references to Psalm 120:1, Psalm 88:6, and Psalm 42:7. While Jonah had rebelled and resisted God's call, we still see great faith in his words as he declares from the belly of the fish that God had heard and answered his cry.

God was not done with Jonah. Jonah knew that it was God who cast him into the sea, not the seamen. God still had a plan to use him to bring a message of repentance to the Ninevites.

Have you ever rebelled or been resistant to God's word? Are you believing any of the enemy's lie that God can't use you? Let's break the power of that lie today. If you've been walking through a time of affliction and you relate to Jonah's prayer, write a prayer below and cry out to the Lord in your distress.

Day One

JONAH 2:1-3

Scripture _____

_____

_____

_____

_____

Observation _____

_____

_____

_____

_____

Application _____

_____

_____

_____

_____

Kneeling in Prayer _____

_____

_____

_____

_____

_____

You brought up my life from the pit.

JONAH 2:6

Jonah describes his experience so eloquently as he details how the waves closed over him, the deep surrounded him, and the weeds wrapped around his head. He describes "the roots of the mountains" and how he "went down to the land". Yet, in all of this we cannot miss the level of faith that he had that God would rescue him and bring him out of the belly of the fish.

In verse 4, Jonah declares "...*yet I shall look again upon your holy temple.*" Despite the horrific experience of being tossed into the sea in the middle of a storm of supernatural proportions and being swallowed up by a giant fish, Jonah **knew** God would bring him out.

This is faith! Do you feel like the waves of life are crashing over you right now? Does it feel like the weeds of tribulation are wrapped around you pulling you further down until it seems like you can literally see the ocean floor of your troubles? Like Jonah do you feel as if the bars are closing around you like a prison cell and you wonder if you will ever be free?

Just like God rescued Jonah from the great fish, just like he rescued the 3 Hebrew men from the fiery furnace, just like he rescued Paul and Silas from prison, he will rescue you! When David was faced with what seemed like an impossible situation, it says in 1 Samuel 30:6 that he strengthened himself in the Lord his God.

What verse or passage of Scripture strengthens you when you are discouraged? Write it below and take extra time to meditate on it this week and strengthen yourself in the Lord your God and let faith grow in your heart that God is on your side, and he is your great deliverer!

_____

_____

_____

_____

_____

_____

_____

_____

Day Two

JONAH 2:4-6

Scripture _____
_____
_____
_____
_____

Observation _____
_____
_____
_____
_____

Application _____
_____
_____
_____
_____

Kneeling in Prayer _____
_____
_____
_____
_____

Salvation belongs to the Lord.

JONAH 2:9

Just when he felt his life was fainting away, Jonah remembered the Lord and cried out to him. Not only was this a frightening experience for Jonah, but it had to have been extremely hot and uncomfortable in the belly of that great fish.

The Hebrew word for idols in this passage of scripture means emptiness or vapor. Indeed, following our ways and assuming we can escape God's hand is empty thinking. Solomon warned us in Proverbs 3 to not lean on our own understanding, but to acknowledge God in all our ways. When we trust in the Lord with our whole heart and acknowledge him in all we do, he will direct our path

In the end, Jonah repented and purposed to fulfill what he had vowed to the Lord. He would take God's message to the Ninevites. He ended his prayer with a victorious declaration, "Salvation belongs to the Lord!"

Perhaps you're in the middle of a battle now. Jonah warned that when we pursue "vain emptiness" we forsake our hope of steadfast love. In other words, we are running from the very thing we need. We need God's stable, unending love. He is our salvation. He will not lead us to destruction, but to hope and a future. You can trust him. He has the very best plans for you.

Have you ever been in a battle for your own will, only to surrender to God in the end? Did you, like Jonah, feel the joyous sense of liberation when you had finally submitted your will to God and purposed to do what he called you to do? Write about it below.

_____

_____

_____

_____

_____

_____

_____

_____

_____

Day Three

JONAH 2:7-9

Scripture _____

_____

_____

_____

_____

Observation _____

_____

_____

_____

_____

_____

Application _____

_____

_____

_____

_____

_____

Kneeling in Prayer _____

_____

_____

_____

_____

_____

_____

And the Lord spoke to the fish, and it vomited Jonah out upon the dry land.

JONAH 2:10

God appointed a great fish to swallow Jonah after he was thrown into the sea. Jonah was in the belly of that fish for three days and nights, where he prayed, repented and thanked God. When he completed his prayer, God spoke to the fish and it vomited Jonah out on to dry ground.

It is so amazing to see God's control over nature in the book of Jonah. So far, we have seen God control the wind, waves, storms and the great fish. In chapter four, we will also see God working through a plant, worm, an east wind and cloudless day. That's our God. He is sovereign over all!

Not only do we see the tremendous hand of God in delivering Jonah from the belly of the great fish, but we also see a foreshadowing of Christ. Jesus said in Matthew 12:40, *"For just as Jonah was three days and three nights in the belly of the great fish, so will the Son of Man be three days and three nights in the heart of the earth."*

Isn't it beautiful the way all of scripture ties together? This is why it is so important to take the time to read all of the books of the Bible. Because our understanding of Jonah gives us a greater understanding of Jesus' words in the book of Matthew.

God is in control. Just as He commands the seas, sets the stars in place, and brings the seasons in perfect rhythm, we can trust that He is sovereign over the details of our lives. Nature does not panic—it follows God's timing. And we can too. Where in life do you need to stop striving and start trusting that God is in control, just as He is with creation?

JONAH 2:10

Scripture _____

_____

_____

_____

_____

_____

Observation _____

_____

_____

_____

_____

_____

Application _____

_____

_____

_____

_____

_____

Kneeling in Prayer _____

_____

_____

_____

_____

Then the word of the Lord came to Jonah a second time.

JONAH 3:1

Though Jonah disobeyed God the first time, God gave him a second chance. Our God is truly a God of second chances! This time Jonah obeyed the word of the Lord and went to Nineveh. The city of Nineveh was an enormous city with huge walls that were over 100 feet high and so wide that three chariots could ride on them side-by-side. In verse three, we see that it took three days to get through this great city.

Surely it had to have been a little intimidating to visit such a great, imposing city and carry this message of God's judgement to a nation that had terrorized your own people. Yet Jonah is ready now to boldly proclaim this prophecy and fulfill the word of the Lord.

Friends, if you feel that you have failed the Lord, remember that failure is a moment in our life, it is not what defines us. God does not relate to us according to our failures but according to his grace. Lamentations 3:22-23 says, "*The steadfast love of the Lord never ceases; his mercies never come to an end; they are new every morning; great is your faithfulness.*"

God is faithful to us, even when we are unfaithful to him. This is the greatest news for mankind. Has there been a time in your life when God gave you a second chance? Take a moment today to reflect on God's faithfulness and mercy to you and give him thanks for all the ways he has given you a second chances.

JONAH 3:1-3

Scripture _____

_____

_____

_____

_____

_____

Observation _____

_____

_____

_____

_____

_____

Application _____

_____

_____

_____

_____

_____

Kneeling in Prayer _____

_____

_____

_____

_____

_____

Week Three

And the people of Nineveh believed God.

JONAH 3:5

It is interesting that the people of Nineveh believed God. It doesn't say they believed Jonah. They recognized Jonah's words as being a word from God. But the city of Nineveh was notorious for its depravity and brutality. It is powerful to think about how the Assyrian people, who were so sinful believed God so rapidly.

It is likely that Jonah's brief declaration, "*Yet forty days, and Nineveh shall be overthrown*" is not the only thing he cried out. However, we don't read that he called the Ninevites to repentance or even gave them any hope that if they did turn from their sin, that God would spare them and their city. However, when they believed God, a fast was proclaimed and all the people put on sackcloth. Sackcloth was a bag-like garment that mourners would put on to signify sorrow and repentance.

The Ninevites immediately believed the word of God that Jonah proclaimed, and yet at that same period two prophets named Hosea and Amos were proclaiming God's warning to the Israelites who refused to obey. The contrast we see between the people of Nineveh and the Israelites is astounding.

Repentance begins with believing what God says about our sin. 1 John 1:9 says, "*If we confess our sins, he is faithful and just to forgive us our sins and to cleanse us from all unrighteousness.*"

Do you have any unconfessed sin in your life today? Confess it to God. He will forgive and cleanse you. He loves you so much!

_____

_____

_____

_____

_____

_____

_____

_____

_____

Day One

JONAH 3:4-5

Scripture _____

_____

_____

_____

_____

Observation _____

_____

_____

_____

_____

_____

Application _____

_____

_____

_____

_____

_____

Kneeling in Prayer _____

_____

_____

_____

_____

_____

God relented of the disaster that he said he would do to them, and he did not do it.

JONAH 3:10

When the king heard about Jonah's message, he stood up, took off his royal garments, put on sackcloth, and sat in ashes. He fully humbled himself and then issued a proclamation throughout the whole city that both man and animal would fast and cry out to God for mercy. He said, "*Who knows? God may turn and relent and turn his fierce anger, so we do not perish.*"

The king also proclaimed, "*Let every man turn from his evil way and from the violence that is in his hands.*" This call for repentance was not just an outward change of behavior, but an inward change of the heart. Repentance is not just changing what we do, but it is changing the way we think about our sin. It's choosing to agree with God about our sin and the seriousness of our disobedience to him.

Our sin may not be to the level of the sin of the Ninevites, but this does not make our sin any less serious to God. He does not overlook small sins anymore than he overlooks big sins. He is a just God, and he must punish sin, or he wouldn't be just. But when we choose to come into agreement with him about sin, he is merciful to us!

God saw the repentance of the Ninevites, and he relented. This does not mean that God changed his mind. The Hebrew word in this verse means that he had compassion upon them, and he chose not to punish them because they repented.

Oh, what great grace and compassion our Father has for us. He loves you so much! In what ways have you experienced God's mercy in your life? Write below about how you have experienced God's compassion.

_____

_____

_____

_____

_____

_____

_____

_____

_____

JONAH 3:6–10

Scripture _____

_____

_____

_____

_____

_____

Observation _____

_____

_____

_____

_____

_____

Application _____

_____

_____

_____

_____

_____

Kneeling in Prayer _____

_____

_____

_____

_____

_____

_____

You are a gracious God and merciful, slow to anger and abounding in steadfast love.

JONAH 4:2

Instead of the book of Jonah ending on a high note, with the happy ending of the city of Nineveh being spared and God's mercy being poured out, it continues. Verse one says that God's mercy toward Nineveh displeased Jonah, and he was angry. Jonah did not go to Nineveh to call the people to repentance, but to eagerly declare that God was going to smite them in his judgement.

Verse two is even more revealing as Jonah lashes out at God. He knew God to be gracious and merciful, so when he heard God's call, he chose to flee to Tarshish because he did not want the Ninevites to have the opportunity to repent. He did not want God to have the opportunity to be merciful to them.

This is how much Jonah hated the Assyrians. He grew so angry that he wanted to die; and God's reply to him was, "*Do you feel you have the right to be angry?*" Jonah had experienced God's forgiveness and mercy yet was unwilling to extend that same forgiveness and mercy to his enemies.

Has there been a time in your life when you witnessed God blessing someone you felt should have experienced consequences instead? Did you, like Jonah, become angry with God that they seemed to escape God's judgement? If you are still upset about this, release that anger to the Lord. Cry out to him and ask him to take away the sting of pain you feel for whatever that person has done and let him fill you with his supernatural love and peace.

Day Three

JONAH 4:1-4

Scripture _____

_____

_____

_____

_____

Observation _____

_____

_____

_____

_____

_____

Application _____

_____

_____

_____

_____

Kneeling in Prayer _____

_____

_____

_____

_____

_____

*Now the LORD God appointed a plant
and made it come up over Jonah,
that it might be a shade over his head,
to save him from his discomfort.*

JONAH 4:6

Still hoping that God would judge the Ninevites, despite his mercy and grace, Jonah left the city and went to a place where he could sit and watch what would happen. As he sat there, God caused a plant to grow that brought shade and a bit of relief from the hot sun. However, the next morning, God caused a worm to attack the plant, and it withered and died. Then God sent a scorching wind, and the sun beat down on him causing him to feel faint.

Once again, Jonah wanted to die. God confronts Jonah a second time with the question, *"Do you have a right to feel angry?"* This time, God is referring to the plant – but perhaps he's not really talking about the plant. God used the plant as an object lesson in Jonah's life to teach him about his sovereignty.

In his pride, Jonah felt justified in his anger towards the Assyrians. They had terrorized his people. He didn't feel they deserved God's mercy. However, he felt he **did** deserve God's mercy so much so that when God caused the plant to die, he felt he had been defrauded in some way. He was a victim of God's injustice.

The Ninevites received a level of God's mercy he did not feel he was being given. It wasn't fair; and God's confrontation was like salt in the wound.

Has there been a time when you felt God wasn't being fair to you? Has there been a situation in which you felt God should have blessed you, but instead of blessing you felt disciplined? Were you angry with God? In what ways has God been merciful to you when you didn't deserve it? Take a moment and thank him for his undeserved love and mercy in your life.

_____

_____

_____

_____

_____

_____

Day Four

JONAH 4:5–9

Scripture _____

_____

_____

_____

_____

_____

Observation _____

_____

_____

_____

_____

_____

Application _____

_____

_____

_____

_____

_____

Kneeling in Prayer _____

_____

_____

_____

_____

_____

And should I not pity Nineveh?

JONAH 4:11

While the final verses of the book of Jonah may seem like a strange ending to this book, they are a powerful illustration of the indescribable depths of God's love and compassion for mankind.

God had sent prophet after prophet to Israel and Judah to warn them of their sinful ways and God's impending judgement. While there had been periods of repentance, their change was not lasting. Eventually both nations would be destroyed and their people carried away into captivity. God had been incredibly long-suffering with his people who had his Law and the prophets to make them aware of their sin.

Nineveh, on the other hand, while certainly not guiltless, did not have God's Law. They did not have prophets who would warn them of their sin. They were hopelessly lost and incapable of escaping God's judgement. In verse ten, God confronts Jonah a third time, explaining to him how he showed more compassion and care for the plant than he did for the 120,000 people of Nineveh who could have been wiped out in God's judgement.

God wanted Jonah to realize the absurdity of his anger about the plant in comparison with his lack of compassion for a city of people who had been created in God's image. It didn't matter to God that they were Gentiles. Though they were enemies of his people, they had believed his word and repented, and God had compassion on them.

This is the indescribable depth of God's love and mercy for us today. Though we have sinned and fallen short of his glory, when we believe his word and repent, he will show his compassion toward us and receive us in his love and mercy.

Do you know someone who needs salvation? Let's close out our study by praying for those in our lives who do not know the Lord yet. Pray that God would give you an opportunity to share with them God's love and mercy, and that they will believe and repent. Keep walking with the King!

Day Five

JONAH 4:10–11

Scripture _____
_____
_____
_____
_____
_____
_____

Observation _____
_____
_____
_____
_____
_____

Application _____
_____
_____
_____
_____
_____

Kneeling in Prayer _____
_____
_____
_____
_____
_____

For Further Reading

STILL STANDING: HOW TO LIVE IN GOD'S LIGHT WHILE WRESTLING WITH THE DARK

by Courtney Joseph Fallick

How do you stand up after life knocks you down?

That's the question Courtney Joseph Fallick asked herself when she entered the darkest season of her life. She found herself drowning in fear, shame, and grief, while God seemed silent.

Opening up about her husband's deep betrayal and abandonment, Courtney shows you how to rise up after your own heart-crushing struggles, cling to God's promises, and move forward stronger than before.

Sharing the hard-fought lessons she learned, she helps you:

- hold on to your faith when life wounds you
- stand back up—and keep standing—after being knocked down
- overcome discouragement and disillusionment
- heal your hurts and let go
- recover from loss and grief
- find enough strength, joy, rest, and peace for each day

This dark valley *will* end. Here is the infusion of hope you need to rise, live well, and walk with the King.

Made in the USA
Coppell, TX
07 June 2025

50423770R00026